IN PROFILE

The War Poets

Christopher Martin

In Profile

Women of the Air
Founders of Religions
Tyrants of the Twentieth Century
Leaders of the Russian Revolution
Pirates and Privateers
Great Press Barons
Explorers on the Nile
Women Prime Ministers
Founders of America
The Cinema Greats
The War Poets
The First Men Round the World

Cover illustration: *Oppy Wood* 1917 by John Nash

First published in 1983 by
Wayland Publishers Ltd
49 Lansdowne Place, Hove
East Sussex BN3 1HF, England

© Copyright 1983 Wayland Publishers Ltd

ISBN 0 85340 886 6

Phototypeset by
Direct Image, Hove, East Sussex
Printed in Italy by
G. Canale & C.S.p.A., Turin
Bound in the U.K. by
The Pitman Press, Bath

Contents

Introduction to the 'soldier poets'   5
Rupert Brooke
   A golden-haired Apollo   7
   The coming of war   14
   The death of Rupert Brooke   17
   Dates and events   19

Siegfried Sassoon
   The voice of protest   21
   A privileged upbringing   23
   Turning against the war   29
   Dates and events   35

Wilfred Owen
   The compassionate poet   36
   Outbreak of war   42
   A year of great poetry   47
   Dates and events   49

Isaac Rosenberg
   Poet and painter against all odds   51
   The art student   55
   Enlistment   57
   Dates and events   61

Glossary   62
Further reading   62
Index   63

Introduction to the 'soldier poets'

The century before the First World War of 1914-18 had produced many poems about warfare. Tennyson's *Charge of the Light Brigade,* about the Crimean War; Walt Whitman's moving *Drum Taps,* about the American Civil War; and Thomas Hardy's verses about the Boer War, are among the greatest.

Most of this poetry had been written by civilians. The soldier poets of the First World War were something different. The huge New Armies, unlike the small professional ones of the nineteenth century, drew in all kinds of men. The result was an amazing range of writing talent. There were ready markets for the work of these war poets. The many papers of the time printed poems to enliven or to contrast with their bleak reports from the Fronts.

Outstanding among hundreds of Great War poets were the four introduced here: Rupert Brooke, who expressed the patriotic enthusiasm of 1914; Siegfried Sassoon, who caught the bitterness and doubt growing after 1916; and Wilfred Owen and Isaac Rosenberg, whose majestic poetry reveals the suffering and waste of the trenches. Whatever the contrasts of their social backgrounds, these poets were united as spokesmen for their tragic generation:

> The unreturning army that was youth;
> The legions who have suffered and are dust.

Opposite *The barrier to advance on the Western Front—'Wire' by Austin Spare.*

Rupert Brooke

A golden-haired Apollo

> Now God be thanked Who has matched us with His hour,
> And caught our youth, and wakened us from sleeping,
> With hand made sure, clear eye, and sharpened power,
> To turn, as swimmers into cleanness leaping,
> Glad from a world grown old and cold and weary . . .
>
> from *Peace* (1915)

By Easter 1915, the sorrow of the First World War, then eight months old, was beginning to bite deeply into British society. Black mourning clothes were to be seen everywhere in the streets. *The Times* of 5th April reported a sermon delivered by Dean Inge in St. Paul's Cathedral, London, on Easter Sunday. It was addressed to the 'thousands of English parents, and young widows, and young orphans, who were thinking of the hastily-made graves in a foreign land, where their dearest are sleeping.' The Dean took his text from Isaiah: 'The dead shall live, my body shall arise.' He had just read a poem on this theme by a young writer, Rupert Brooke, whose sonnet, *The Soldier*, had recently been published. It began:

> If I should die, think only this of me:
> That there's some corner of a foreign field
> That is forever England . . .

'Pure and elevated patriotism had never found a nobler expression,' concluded the Dean.

Brooke read this report on 18th April, aboard ship in the Mediterranean. Twenty-seven years old, he was

7

Rupert (right) with his brother Alfred, who also died in the First World War.

about to take part in the attack on Turkish-held Gallipoli. He never saw action. On 23rd April he died, victim of blood poisoning following a mosquito bite.

Brooke's friend, Winston Churchill, then First Lord of the Admiralty, wrote about him in *The Times*: 'A voice had become audible, a note had been struck, more true, more thrilling, more able to do justice to the nobility of our youth in arms . . . than any other . . . The voice has been swiftly stilled.'

The Dean's sermon and Churchill's moving words turned Rupert Brooke into a national hero: the typical young volunteer patriot, who willingly gave his life for his country. Heroes and ideals were badly needed in 1915, to justify mounting casualties and to help console the bereaved. Brooke's war sonnets caught the mood of

Rugby School, where Rupert's father was a housemaster.

the time, and they sold in thousands. It seemed that he would become, as one journalist suggested, 'a mythical figure, a legend almost.'

Rugby and Cambridge

The reality behind this 'mythical figure' was less simple and more interesting. Rupert Chawner Brooke was born on 3rd August 1887. His father was a housemaster at Rugby, the boy's public school made famous by the Victorian novel, *Tom Brown's Schooldays*.

In 1901, Rupert joined his father's House, School Field. He loved the school where, he said, 'every hour was golden and radiant.' His charm, vitality and all-round ability at work and games made him very popular. He was good enough at classics (Latin and Greek, which were then the basis of public school study) to win a Cambridge Scholarship in 1906. What he loved most, however, was to explore English literature on his own in the school library. A writer friend of the family introduced him to some of the poets of the 1890s, like Swinburne and Ernest Dowson. His first schoolboy poems imitate their dreamy vagueness. He also copied the mannerisms of the 'Nineties' poets, growing his red-gold hair rather long. Already people in the street turned to stare at his extraordinary good looks, which are so much a part of his legend.

In 1906, Rupert went up to King's College, Cambridge, where he found new interests. He helped found the Marlowe Dramatic Society, which performed Elizabethan plays. Although his acting was described as awkward and his voice as thick and indistinct, he made a great impression as a herald in a Greek play, in a red wig and cardboard armour.

A second interest was Fabian socialism. The Fabian Society, led by Sidney and Beatrice Webb, believed that social injustices should be cured by gradual reform, after careful study, rather than by sudden revolution. Rupert attended Fabian meetings and summer schools, less impressed by statistics than by more colourful socialist

Rupert playing the part of a herald in a Greek play at Cambridge.

King's College, Cambridge, where Rupert studied.

texts, like *New Worlds for Old*, written by his friend, the 'wee, fantastic' H. G. Wells. Rupert's socialism was always rather sentimental. Another friend, the novelist, Virginia Woolf, said he liked to believe 'that there was something deep and wonderful in the man who brought the milk and the woman who watched the cows.'

These activities brought Rupert many new admirers. To young and middle-aged, to male and female, he was 'A young Apollo, golden-haired.' 'It was a continual pleasure to look at him fresh each day,' a friend wrote of him. 'He seemed like a symbol of youth for all time.' Rupert came to love the open air life that had been adopted by progressive young Cambridge Edwardians, 'the dew dabblers', as they were called. He camped, swam naked, walked barefoot and sang round the fire.

Rupert continued to write poems for literary magazines. Under the influence of the Jacobean poet, John Donne, who was then attracting interest, he developed a new, plain, conversational style. This is seen in a poem, written in 1907, which describes an uncomfortable Italian train journey:

> The darkness shivers. A wan light through the rain
> Strikes on our faces, drawn and white. Somewhere
> A new day sprawls; and, inside, the foul air
> Is chill, and damp, and fouler than before . . .
> Opposite me two Germans sweat and snore.

Rupert writing in the garden of the Old Vicarage, Grantchester.

Rowing on the River Granta, during student days at Cambridge.

Part of the manuscript for 'The Old Vicarage, Grantchester', which Rupert wrote in Berlin.

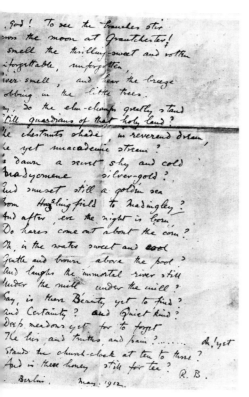

Grantchester

With so many distractions, the poet only managed a second-class in his University Classical Tripos examinations of 1909. To make amends, he began work on a thesis about the Jacobean dramatist, John Webster. He hoped this might earn him a Fellowship at King's College. He sought quieter lodgings at Grantchester, a village on the river Granta, a few miles from Cambridge. From here the beautiful spires of King's College were visible over the trees. It was a pleasant walk, cycle ride or canoe trip into town.

Rupert lodged at the Old Vicarage, a large, ramshackle house, where he had three rooms. He loved the overgrown garden, running down to the river, which he described as 'a paradise of scent and colour'. Here, in 1911, he spent the happiest summer of his life, writing or reciting verse to his friends on the lawn, lounging in a canoe to make notes, or walking through the white dusty lanes to swim in nearby Byron's Pool. He caught the magic of the place in his most popular poem, *The Old Vicarage, Grantchester,* composed in a Berlin cafe in 1912.

In December 1911, Rupert's first collection of poems was published. The critics thought his poems showed promise, though many disliked his realistic style. *A Channel Passage* caused an uproar. It was about a young man crossing to France, unhappy in love and tormented by sea-sickness.

> Now there's a choice—heartache or tortured liver!
> A sea-sick body, or a you-sick soul!
> Do I forget you? Retchings twist and tie me,
> Old meat, good meals, brown gobbets up I throw.

This 'disgusting sonnet . . . ought never to have been published,' said *The Times* critic.

Among those who praised the book was Edward Marsh, an important civil servant, then acting as Winston Churchill's Private Secretary. Marsh was quite rich and used his money to help young poets and painters. Rupert became a frequent visitor to his rooms

The Old Vicarage, Grantchester, as it is today.

Rupert photographed with a group of friends, when he visited the South Sea islands in 1914.

in Gray's Inn, London, and, through Marsh, met leading political and artistic figures of the day. In September 1912, the two men, disappointed that good modern poets were not widely known, planned a collection of Georgian poetry (George V having just become King). Clear and readable, *Georgian Poetry 1911-12* was an enormous success. It, and others in the series, dominated poetic taste for ten years, selling thousands of copies.

At Cambridge, Rupert had fallen in love with a Newnham undergraduate, Katherine ('Ka') Cox. By 1912, their uneasy romance had caused distress on both sides, bringing Rupert to the verge of a nervous breakdown, 'a foodless and sleepless hell.' As he recovered, he was glad to plunge into a brilliant London round of parties and dinners. He loved the colour and excitement of two theatre shows, the jazz review *Hello Ragtime* which he saw ten times, and the sensational Russian Ballet which he saw fifteen times! He also met a beautiful young actress, Cathleen Nesbitt, who became the centre of his ill-starred emotional life.

America and the Pacific

Rupert's thesis on Webster's plays finally won him his longed-for Fellowship at King's in March 1913. Exhausted and still restless, he set off for a year's travel in America. The *Westminster Gazette* had asked him to do a series of articles recording his impressions of American life. As he passed from New York and Boston,

The island of Tahiti, which Rupert loved, and where he wrote a poem 'Tiare Tahiti', dedicated to a Tahitian girl.

through Canada to San Francisco, he wrote with grace and skill about his experiences.

In October, on impulse, he continued across the Pacific into the South Seas, travelling from Hawaii and Samoa to New Zealand, and finally to Tahiti. He was enchanted by the islands. Samoa was 'sheer beauty, so pure that it is difficult to breathe in it.' He delighted in the people: 'How far nearer the Kingdom of Heaven—or the Garden of Eden—these good, naked, laughing people are than oneself.' He lingered in Tahiti, 'the most ideal place in the world', having found a native sweetheart, Taata Mata, to whom he addressed his charming poem, *Tiare Tahiti*.

> Crown the hair, and come away
> Hear the calling of the moon,
> And the whispering scents that stray
> About the idle warm lagoon.
> Hasten, hand in human hand,
> Down the dark, the flowered way,
> Along the whiteness of the sand . . .

The Coming of War

By June 1914, Brooke was back in England. Siegfried Sassoon met 'the wonderful Rupert' in Edward Marsh's flat. He 'hadn't bothered to brush his brown-gold hair,' recalled Sassoon. 'His eyes were a living blue and his face was still sunburnt.' Here was 'one on whom had been conferred all the visible attributes of a poet.'

As the European crisis deepened in July, Rupert became uneasy about 'this damned war business.' Should he enlist or become a war correspondent? 'It will be Hell to be in it; and Hell to be out of it,' he wrote to a friend. After fighting began, he was moved by 'those people at the Front who are fighting muddledly enough for some idea called England—it's a faint shadowing of goodness and loveliness they have in their hearts to die for.'

His contact with Winston Churchill eventually won him a commission in a new unit, the Royal Naval Division. By late September, Rupert was in camp in Kent, finding 'incredible beauty . . . at night under a full moon, faint lights blurring through the ghostly tents, and a distant bugle blowing Lights Out.'

In early October, the swift German advance towards Antwerp in Belgium sent the Division across the Channel and into battle. In the 'thrilling confusion' of this first taste of war, Rupert was excited to find himself brave under fire in the trenches. There were, he told Cathleen Nesbitt, 'incessant thunders . . . and, above, recurrent wailings, very shrill and queer like lost souls, crossing and recrossing the emptiness . . . Once or twice a lovely glittering aeroplane, very high up, would go over us.'

The line collapsed, and they marched away along the river, spectacular with flame and smoke from burning petrol tanks on its banks. Rupert was haunted by the trailing figures of thousands of refugees, lit up by this glare. His experience of war's 'frightfulness' sharpened his fear for England, and his determination to 'get good at beating Germans.'

Rupert with the poet Frances Cornford, picnicking in Norfolk on the day Britain and Germany went to war, 4th August 1914.

War sonnets and the Dardanelles

Back in camp in Dorset, he began to write his five war sonnets. After a Christmas Day looking after drunken stokers, he drafted *The Soldier*. It was 'turning out fairly,' he told a friend. 'It's rather like developing photographs.' By January 1915, his 'five camp children' were finished and sent to his poet friend, Wilfrid Gibson, for publication in the poetry magazine, *New Numbers*. If *The Soldier* is best known, *Peace* caught the mood of the time most vividly. It echoes Shakespeare's line in *Henry V*: 'Now all the youth of England are on fire':

> Now God be thanked Who has matched us with His hour
> And caught our youth, and wakened us from sleeping . . .

The poem also reflects the sense of purpose that war had given to the poet's own rather aimless life.

In February 1915, Rupert heard that the Naval Division was to take part in an assault on the Turkish-held Dardanelles Straits in the Eastern Mediterranean. Turkey, Germany's ally, was to be smashed, and a way opened to the Black Sea ports of Russia, Britain's ally. The poet struck one of his many poses in his excitement: 'Shall we be a Turning Point in history? Oh God! I've never been quite so happy.' Violet Asquith, the Prime

15

The sentimental view of dying for England: 'The Last Message' by W. Hatherell.

A group of officers in the Royal Naval Division—Rupert is standing, second from the left.

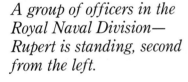

Minister's daughter, watched his departure from Avonmouth—marines playing a salute on silver trumpets as the ship sailed on 28th February. The decks were 'crowded with young, splendid figures, happy, resolute and confident,' she wrote.

Rupert Brooke's last letters described the joys of the voyage: 'The sea and sky are all the colours of a peacock or a rainbow.' The classical scholar in him thrilled to a first sight of Greece. Dark threads of regret—that he had never married, that he had no child, that 'there's some bad luck about me'—were also apparent. Thoughts of death are the theme of a moving fragment composed on the voyage. He watched his friends through the cabin windows:

> I could but see them—against the lamplight—pass
> Like coloured shadows, thinner than filmy glass,
> Slight bubbles, fainter than the far wave's faint light,
> That broke to phosphorus out in the night,
> Perishing things and strange ghosts—soon to die
> To other ghosts—this one, or that, or I.

After resting at the Allied Base at Lemnos, the Division took part in a feint attack on the Gallipoli peninsula that overlooked the Dardanelles. This was the poet's last view of the War: 'We paraded in silence under paling stars . . . The darkness on the sea was full of scattered flashing lights . . . Slowly the day became wan and green and the sea opal. Everyone's face looked drawn and ghastly . . .'

The death of Rupert Brooke

In April they sailed to Port Said in Egypt to rest. In a dismal, hot, sand-swept camp, Rupert contracted sunstroke and dysentry. He was troubled, too, by a swollen lip, caused by a mosquito bite.

When the Division returned to Lemnos, he was feeling better. On 20th April, there was a field exercise on the nearby island of Skyros, connected in Greek legend with Theseus and Achilles. In the afternoon, Brooke and his friends rested in an olive grove, a place of 'extraordinary beauty . . . Rupert liked the place and spoke of it,' noted Denis Browne, an old school friend and fellow officer.

Rupert's lip swelled again. Soon doctors diagnosed acute blood poisoning. He was transferred to a hospital ship for an operation, but gradually faded, and died on 23rd April.

Brooke's funeral had the same pathos and glamour as the poet Shelley's cremation on an Italian beach nearly a century before. His friends, due to sail for Gallipoli next morning, carried him laboriously to the olive grove. His grave was lined with flowers, and an olive wreath placed on the coffin. He was buried by moonlight to the sound of the Last Post. Large pieces of pink and white marble

The last picture taken of Rupert Brooke, lying ill outside his tent, in Egypt 1915.

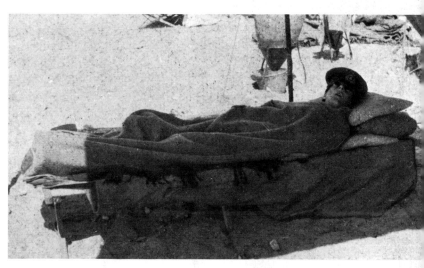

Rupert's grave on the Greek island of Skyros.

Rupert Brooke's memorial in Rugby School Chapel.

RUPERT BROOKE
1887–1915
IF I SHOULD DIE, THINK ONLY THIS OF ME :
THAT THERE'S SOME CORNER OF A FOREIGN FIELD
THAT IS FOREVER ENGLAND. THERE SHALL BE
IN THAT RICH EARTH A RICHER DUST CONCEALED ;
A DUST WHOM ENGLAND BORE, SHAPED, MADE AWARE,
GAVE, ONCE, HER FLOWERS TO LOVE, HER WAYS TO ROAM ;
A BODY OF ENGLAND'S, BREATHING ENGLISH AIR,
WASHED BY HER RIVERS, BLEST BY SUNS OF HOME .
AND THINK, THIS HEART, ALL EVIL SHED AWAY,
A PULSE IN THE ETERNAL MIND, NO LESS   GIVEN ;
GIVES SOMEWHERE BACK THE THOUGHTS BY ENGLAND
HER SIGHTS & SOUNDS ; DREAMS HAPPY AS HER DAY ;
AND LAUGHTER, LEARNT OF FRIENDS ; & GENTLENESS,
IN HEARTS AT PEACE, UNDER AN ENGLISH HEAVEN.

were piled up around the white wooden cross that carried his name.

Denis Browne passed Skyros in June, on his way to his own death at Gallipoli: 'Every colour had come into the sea and sky to do him honour; and it seemed that the island must ever be shining with his glory that we buried there.'

The cult for soldiers' verse

The apparent romance of Brooke's death and the success of the sonnets created a fashion for 'soldier poets'. A writer later remembered how, in 1915, 'lying about in every smart London drawing room you would find the latest little volume, and at every fashionable bookshop, the half-crown war poets were among the best-selling lines.' Not all of their verse is good, yet the sheer skill of many young scholars trained in classical

verse-making, and carrying thin-paper editions of *The Oxford Book of English Verse* in their packs at the Front, did produce moving poetry about patriotic sacrifice. A memorial poem from Marlborough College magazine catches the spirit of Brooke's fine attitudes:

Farewell, young king, away you fling,
All in the flush of youth,
Playing the game, the grand last game
For England and for Truth.

This 1917 cover of 'The Bookman' reflects the huge sales of Brooke's poems.

Dates and events

1887 Born at Rugby, England (3rd August).

1901 Enters Rugby School where his father was a Housemaster.

1906 Goes to King's College, Cambridge with a classical scholarship. New interests in Fabian socialism and drama.

1909 Second class Honours in Classical Tripos examination.

1910 Moves to the Old Vicarage, Grant-chester. Begins work on thesis about the playwright John Webster.

1911 First collection of poems published.

1912 Nervous breakdown following unhappy love affair with Ka Cox. Writes *The Old Vicarage, Grant-chester* in a Berlin cafe. Prepares *Georgian Poetry* collection with Edward Marsh.

1913 Wins Fellowship at King's College, Cambridge. Leaves for year tour of United States, Canada and Pacific, contributing articles to *Westminster Gazette*.

1914 Visits Pacific Islands. Writes *Tiare Tahiti*. Returns to England (June). War with Germany declared (4th August). Commissioned officer in Royal Naval Division (Sept.). Takes part in unsuccessful defence of Antwerp in Belgium (Oct.). Writes the five war sonnets (Dec.).

1915 War sonnets published in the poetry magazine *New Numbers*. Sails for Mediterranean to take part in Dardanelles Campaign (February). Reaches Allied base at Lemnos in Greece (March). Dean Inge's quotation from *The Soldier* during St. Paul's sermon makes Brooke famous (5th April). Brooke dies of blood poisoning. Buried on the Greek Island of Skyros (23rd April). Winston Churchill writes his obituary in *The Times* (26th April). *1914 and Other poems* published.

1918 *Collected Poems* (with Memoir by Edward Marsh) published.

Glyn Philpot 1917

Siegfried Sassoon

The voice of protest

The place was rotten with dead; green clumsy legs,
High-booted, sprawled and grovelled along the saps;
And trunks, face downward in the sucking mud,
Wallowed like trodden sand-bags loosely filled;
And naked sodden buttocks, mats of hair,
Bulged, clotted heads slept in the plastering slime.

from *Counter Attack* (1918)

By 1917, the war in Europe had become a stalemate. The Western Front, a maze of trenches 450 miles long, wound its way from the Swiss border to the North Sea. It was a nightmare world of mud, shell-holes and broken trees.

During the day, soldiers crouched between trench walls, resting as best they could, tormented by extremes of weather, by lice, fleas and huge rats, and by bullets and shells that brought them sudden death or hideous wounds. At night, they toiled at fatigues, dragging up supplies or mending the tangled fences of barbed wire that protected their trenches. Or they crawled out to patrol No-Man's Land between the opposing lines.

The weapons of defence—the machine-gun, artillery fire and barbed wire—were stronger than the weapons of attack. No army could break the trench deadlock until 1918, although huge offensives were launched each year.

In 1916, the British Army attacked on the Somme. Casualties were horrific as, wrote Winston Churchill, generals were 'content to fight machine-gun bullets with the breasts of gallant men.' 57,470 men were killed or

'A sketch for Menin Road, near Ypres', by the painter Paul Nash, who described the Flanders battlefields as 'one huge grave . . . '

wounded on the Battle's first day, the notorious 1st July.

In 1917, the battle of Passchendaele was fought in rain and sucking mud, with more heavy losses. The artist Paul Nash described the battlefield: 'The rain drives on, the stinking mud becomes more evilly yellow, the shell-holes fill up with green-white water, the black dying trees ooze and sweat and the shells never cease . . . This land (is) one huge grave and cast upon it the poor dead. It is unspeakable, godless, hopeless.'

The British Army never broke into the widespread mutiny that threatened other armies in 1917. There were resentments among soldiers: of staff officers at Army Headquarters, living comfortably while they planned battles in a front line they rarely saw; of journalists who lied about the fighting; of profiteers who flourished in wartime; of armchair patriots who glorified the excitements and horrors of a war in which they played no active part. There were also doubts, not only about the conduct of the war, but about its very purpose. What exactly were men fighting for?

The anger and doubt growing among soldiers during the later war years were given their most memorable expression in the savage trench poems of Sassoon's.

Opposite *Siegfried (centre) with his father and brothers.*

A privileged upbringing

Siegfried Sassoon was born in Kent on 8th September 1886. On his father's side he was descended from a wealthy Jewish banking family which had made a name in Victorian politics and high society. Siegfried's great-uncle Reuben had been a close friend of Edward, Prince of Wales. On his mother's side, he was related to several talented Victorian artists, engineers and writers.

In his book, *The Old Century*, Sassoon recreated his golden childhood in this rich, cultivated background. The garden of his large home overlooked the Weald of Kent, which he described as 'an easy-going prospect of meadow, orchards, and hop gardens.' In such delightful surroundings, Siegfried and his brothers were raised by his mother and various tutors. There was one shadow: when he was five, his father left home, and later died in 1895.

Siegfried's devoted mother encouraged her son's early interest in poetry, believing he would be a great poet. When he was eleven, he gave her a collection of his poems for Christmas, hand-written and coloured. They were not very cheerful poems: 'Eternity and the Tomb were among my favourite themes,' he wrote later.

At Marlborough College, where he went in 1902, Siegfried made no particular mark. He began to collect books, and developed those sporting interests, in cricket, golf and riding, that were to be his passion in later life. After school, he went to Clare College, Cambridge, where he listlessly studied law and history, leaving without a degree.

Wealthy enough to live without a profession, Siegfried returned home to devote himself to country pleasures, especially fox hunting and point-to-point racing. His only ambition in this comfortable existence was to be 'a really good poet.'

Poetry was a private hobby for him. In the years after Cambridge he published, at his own expense, several little booklets of his work. Siegfried's over-protected, narrow life gave him few real subjects to write about. Like many young Edwardian poets, he wrote in a style of beautiful, high-minded vagueness, in the fashion of the

Clare College, Cambridge, where Siegfried was an unenthusiastic student.

As a young man, Siegfried loved fox hunting.

poets of the late Victorian era. A typical early Sassoon line was 'Old days that are filled with the fragrance of dreams.'

In December 1912, he made a breakthrough. The poet John Masefield had written *The Everlasting Mercy*, a story of working people, written in their own language, which had become the most popular poem of the time. Siegfried did an imitation, *The Daffodil Murderer*. His poem had enough life of its own, and real observation of Sussex, for him to claim that he had found 'a new pair of poetic legs.'

> And as they lead me to the gallows
> I'll think of peewits in the fallows,
> Flapping their wings and sadly calling
> Because it's cold and twilight's falling.

The poem attracted the attention and praise of Edward Marsh who, in 1912 had planned a collection of Georgian Poetry with Rupert Brooke. In 1913, Siegfried came to live in London, renting rooms near Marsh's flat. Here, in the last months of peace, he went again and again to the visiting Russian Opera and Ballet, and met and talked with other writers, like Brooke and the remarkable tramp poet, W. H. Davies.

Siegfried enlisted as a trooper three days before the outbreak of War, but later obtained a commission in the Royal Welch Fusiliers.

First taste of war

Having heard in late July 1914 that war was inevitable, Siegfried decided to enlist at once. On 1st August, therefore, three days before Britain declared war, he cycled into Tunbridge Wells to join the Sussex Yeomanry. He slept the night on the Town Hall floor, and was already wearing his 'ill-fitting khaki' on the first morning of the War. His life seemed to have fresh purpose: 'It seemed almost as if I had been waiting for this to happen,' he wrote later.

At first he enjoyed the open-air life in the beautiful late summer of 1914. As a trooper, he was teased by officers who had been former hunting friends. Less pleasant was to see his own horses commandeered by the Army. A fall which broke his arm ended his brief Yeomanry experience, and in early 1915, helped by an old soldier friend of his mother, he obtained a commission in the Royal Welch Fusiliers.

In April Siegfried began training at the Depot in Litherland, near Liverpool. The ugly camp was a 'soldier manufactory', full of the sounds of bugle calls, shouted commands and marching feet. He found acquaintances would suddenly vanish, having been drafted to the Fronts. The real War began 'to lay a wiry finger on the heart.'

Soon, in November, it was Siegfried's turn. He joined the First Battalion near Festubert in France. He met a fellow soldier poet, Robert Graves, with whom he discussed writing. At this stage Siegfried disliked his friend's realistic war poems and still preferred to write poetry in the heroic style. A poem written in memory of his brother, killed recently at Gallipoli, was in this manner:

> But in the gloom I see your laurell'd head
> And through your victory I shall win the light.

Late in 1915, the Battalion moved south to take up a new line position near the River Somme. Here the great Battle of 1916 was to be fought. Siegfried enjoyed

'Over the top' by John Nash: attacking on the Front Line, to which Siegfried went in November 1915.

himself riding a black mare about the countryside. But when a close friend was killed in the trenches, he became angry and began to show the reckless courage for which he became well known. To revenge his friend he volunteered to patrol the mine craters near Fricourt, hoping to kill a German. In June 1916, during a raid on German trenches at Mametz, he won the Military Cross for rescuing a wounded man under heavy fire. Its purple and white ribbon became his proudest possession.

On 1st July, the Battle of the Somme began, and Siegfried, from a reserve position, watched the huge attack. He noted in his diary: 'The sunlight flashes on bayonets as the tiny figures move quietly forward . . . I am staring at a sunlit picture of Hell.' Next day Siegfried

'Gassed and wounded' by E. Kennington. Siegfried was haunted by the delirium of a Somme victim, when he was sent to hospital in Amiens.

joined the advance through captured German positions, horrified by the heaps of dead. Mametz Wood, dense and dangerous, loomed ahead as a barrier to further progress. When one of his men was shot by a sniper, Siegfried, clutching a bag of bombs, went forward alone, driving a crowd of Germans from a trench by the wood. Although he could not hold his capture single-handed, he fought all morning with a desperate courage.

Later in July, he fell ill from gastric fever. In hospital at Amiens, he was haunted by the delirium of another Somme victim. This experience caused him to write the poem *Died of Wounds*:

> The ward grew dark; but he was still complaining
> And calling out for 'Dickie'. 'Curse the Wood!
> 'It's time to go. O Christ, and what's the good?
> 'We'll never take it, and it's always raining!'

'All the horror of the Somme attacks was in that raving,' Siegfried wrote in *Memoirs of an Infantry Officer*. 'All the darkness and the dreadful daylight.'

Turning against the War

As he recovered in an Oxford hospital, Siegfried's war experiences began to pour out in the first of his angry war poems. He suddenly discovered a new way of writing, using slangy, everyday English, with a pattern of sharp rhymes leading to a 'knockout blow' in the last verse. A hint from a newspaper or a memory of France would 'bring poems into my head, as though from nowhere.' He aimed to shock complacent civilians. So, *The Hero* exposes the emptiness of a popular phrase like 'the supreme sacrifice', which was often used to justify and glorify a soldier's death. In the poem Jack's mother is told about her dead 'glorious boy'. A fellow soldier recalls what he was really like:

> He thought how 'Jack', cold-footed, useless swine,
> Had panicked down the trench that night the mine
> Went up at Wicked Corner; how he'd tried
> To get sent home, and how, at last, he died
> Blown to small bits . . .

These first savage satires, were aimed to strike at 'blood-thirsty civilians, . . . and those who falsely glorified the War.' When they appeared in *The Old Huntsman* in 1917, they startled readers because they were something entirely new.

Siegfried returned to France in February 1917, in time for the British offensive at Arras in April. He described the sinister details of the fighting in *Memoirs of an Infantry Officer*: 'a pair of hands . . . which protruded from the soaked ashen soil like the roots of a tree turned upside down.' In the dark tunnels under a captured German trenchline, he found, lit by his torch: 'The livid face of a dead German whose fingers still clutched the blackened gash on his neck.' After another brave bombing exploit, Siegfried was shot through the shoulder. and again sent home.

He was now deeply distressed in mind and probably shell-shocked. He lay in his hospital bed at night, imagining that 'shapes of mutilated soldiers came crawling across the floor' which 'seemed to be littered with fragments of mangled flesh.' His anti-war poems

TAKE UP THE SWORD OF JUSTICE

Sassoon's protests were directed against glorification of the War, as expressed by this recruiting poster.

became more critical of the people in authority, who sent thousands of men to futile slaughter while they remained safe. *The General* (reproduced left) is a typical example. In *Base Details:* he again attacks those in authority:

> If I were fierce, and bald, and short of breath,
> I'd live with scarlet Majors at the Base,
> And speed glum heroes up the line to death.

A statement of protest

By July 1917, Siegfried had come to share H. G. Wells' opinion that the War was now 'without a point . . . It has become mere incoherent fighting and destruction.' He planned some form of personal protest against it.

He had met leading British pacifists at Garsington Manor, near Oxford, the home of the eccentric Lady Ottoline Morrell, wife of a Liberal M.P. He had no sympathy for the 'conscientious objectors', who did so-called war work on the manor estate. But he did admire Bertrand Russell, the brilliant philosopher and mathematician, who was later sent to prison for his pacifist opinions. Through the Morrells, he also met H. W. Massingham, the editor of a weekly magazine, *The Nation.*

Talking with Massingham, Siegfried was angry to hear of the diplomatic scheming that was prolonging the War. He took up Massingham's hint that if the fighting soldier spoke out against the conflict, it could not last a month. He now considered making a statement of protest. This was a very courageous action to take: the result for him would be a court-martial, disgrace and prison.

Bertrand Russell helped Siegfried to draft the statement. In mid-July it was posted to his Commanding Officer. Then it was made public in the newspapers. 'I have seen and endured the sufferings of the troops,' wrote Sassoon, 'and I can no longer be a party to prolong those sufferings for ends which I believe to be evil and

THE GENERAL.

'Good-morning; good-morning!' the General said
When we met him last week on our way to the Line.
Now the soldiers he smiled at are most of 'em dead,
And we're cursing his staff for incompetent swine.
'He's a cheery old card', grunted Harry to Jack
As they slogged up to Arras with rifle and pack.

*   *   *

But he did for them both by his plan of attack.

Manuscript of Sassoon's poem, 'The General' from 'Counter Attack'.

unjust.' He continued to say that the War was being prolonged by cynical governments, and soldiers were the victims of their policies.

A question about the statement was asked in Parliament, and the case was hotly debated in the press. Siegfried's friend and fellow-poet Robert Graves, who had been shocked by the statement, used his influence to prevent a court martial.

Sassoon was told to remain in a Liverpool hotel while his case was discussed. After several sleepless nights, he went out to the nearby coast, tore the Military Cross ribbon from his tunic and threw it in the river Mersey.

At a special Medical Board, Graves spoke for Sassoon, pleading a nervous breakdown. The authorities, glad to end an embarrassment, sent him to a hospital for shell-shocked officers at Craiglockhart, near Edinburgh.

Craiglockhart and 'Counter Attack'

The hospital was a melancholy place, not unpleasant by day when amusements and sports were arranged for the patients. 'But at night,' Sassoon wrote later, 'it was very different'. 'One lay awake and listened to feet padding along passages . . . The place was full of men whose slumbers were morbid and terrifying, men muttering uneasily and suddenly crying out in their sleep . . . Each man was back in his doomed sector of a horror-

Sassoon was sent to a hospital for shell-shocked officers, after publishing his statement of protest about the conduct of the War.

31

'A German gas attack' and 'Trench Suicide' by the German artist Otto Dix. These gruesome drawings illustrate the futility of war, reflected in Sassoon's bitter, satirical war poems.

stricken front line where the panic and stampede of some ghastly experience was re-enacted among the livid faces of the dead.' At the hospital the poet was guided back to health by a distinguished doctor, W. H. Rivers. Here, too, he met and influenced another patient and war-poet, Wilfred Owen. Both men published poems in the hospital magazine, *The Hydra*.

Siegfried began collecting the poems eventually published in *Counter Attack*. When the book appeared in 1918, it caused a sensation. 'Cries of pain wrung from soldiers during a test to destruction,' Winston Churchill called it. More enduring, perhaps, than the angry poems are those pictures of the trenches, 'the hell where youth and laughter go.' There are soldiers:

> Disconsolate men who stamp their sodden boots
> And turn dulled, sunken faces to the sky
> Haggard and hopeless . . .

and landscapes:

> Sad, smoking, flat horizons, reeking woods
> And foundered trench lines volleying doom for doom.

The poem allows us to share the near insanity induced by battle, among:

> The strangled horror
> And butchered, frantic gestures of the dead.

'The unreturning army'—soldier silhouettes, Arras 1917.

His war poems turned Siegfried into a celebrity. He now met as an equal many of the great literary figures of the time, including his personal hero, Thomas Hardy. Always a shy man, he found it hard to read his poems at society parties. As he read, noted another war poet, Robert Nichols, he had 'the air of a sullen falcon . . . He speaks slowly, in a voice that has something of the troubled thickness apparent in the voices of those who emerge from a deep grief.'

France and the Armistice

In February, 1918, Siegfried Sassoon returned yet again to active service, going first to Egypt and Palestine, then, in May, to France to help stem the German advance of that spring. On 13th July, after another daring patrol into No-Man's Land, he was shot in

A drawing of Sassoon by Max Beerbohm.

the head, accidentally by one of his own men. It was not a serious injury, but enough to end Sassoon's War.

At eleven o'clock on the quiet grey morning of 11th November 1918, Siegfried, walking in the fields near Garsington, heard the victory bells and saw flags fluttering from cottage windows. The Armistice had come; the War was over. He had survived. His poem, *Everyone Sang* was a celebration:

> My heart was shaken with tears; and horror
> Drifted away.

The poet lived on until 1967, winning new fame with his brilliant autobiographies and writing many more poems. But he never recovered the power of his war satires, those 'trench rockets sent up to illuminate the gloom.' It was Sassoon, said H. G. Wells, who best summed up the tragedy of the Great War: 'His song is a cry of anger at the old men who have led the world to destruction. Youth turns upon age . . . saying, "What is this to which you have brought us? What have you done with our lives?" '

Dates and events

1886 Born in Kent, England (8th September).

1902 Goes to Marlborough College, after home tuition by governess and tutor.

1906 Reads Law and History at Clare College, Cambridge. Leaves without a degree. With substantial private means, he devotes himself to poetry and outdoor sports.

1913 His imitation of Masefield, *The Daffodil Murderer* creates interest. Meets Edward Marsh, patron of Georgian poets. Takes rooms near Marsh in London.

1914 1st August: enlists in Sussex Yeomanry before outbreak of war. Home Service as a trooper ended by fall from horse which breaks his arm.

1915 April: begins training as Second Lieutenant in Royal Welch Fusiliers at Litherland Camp, Liverpool, England. November: crosses to France. First taste of trench warfare on La Bassée section of Western Front.

1916 June: wins Military Cross during trench raid on Somme section. July: takes part in Battle of the Somme, showing outstanding courage at Mametz Wood. Falls ill with gastric fever: invalided home. Begins to write war satires (first published in *The Old Huntsman*, May 1917).

1917 February: returns to France. April: takes part in Battle of Arras. Wounded by a sniper: sent home. July: after encouragement from leading pacifists, Sassoon makes public his statement of protest against the war. Robert Graves pleads for his friend at a Military Medical Board. Sassoon declared shell-shocked and sent to recover at Craiglockhart Hospital, Edinburgh. August: meets and influences Wilfred Owen, fellow-patient and war poet.

1918 February: returns to active service in Palestine and (in May) France. June: *Counter Attack and other poems*: Sassoon's finest war poetry. 13th July: wounded in the head and returns to England. End of war service. 11th November: end of the Great War.

1928 *Memoirs of a Fox-hunting Man* published.

1930 *Memoirs of an Infantry Officer* published.

1936 *Sherston's Progress* published.

1957 Joins Catholic Church. Awarded Queen's Medal for Poetry.

1967 Death of Siegfried Sassoon (Sept.)

Wilfred Owen

The com- passionate poet

The front line withers,
But they are troops who fade, not flowers
For poets' tearful fooling:
Men, gaps for filling:
Losses, who might have fought
Longer; but no one bothers.

from *Insensibility* (1918)

For the opening of the new Coventry Cathedral in 1962, the composer Benjamin Britten was commissioned to write his *War Requiem.* Here the traditional words of the Catholic Mass were set against a sequence of war poems by Wilfred Owen. This was very appropriate. The Cathedral was built beside the ruins of the old one, destroyed, like most of the city centre, in the terrible German air raid of 1940. Nevertheless, the theme of the new building was reconciliation between former enemies. This same Christian idea is prominent in one of Wilfred Owen's most celebrated poems, *Strange Meeting.* The poet imagines that, having died in battle, he finds himself in Hell, a 'profound, dull tunnel', like a giant trench dug-out.

No blood reached there from the upper ground,
And no guns thumped, or down the flues made moan.

Men line the walls of the tunnel, sunk in uneasy sleep. One springs up, recognizing the poet. This man, too, was a writer, who, like Owen, had intended to write great prophetic poems about

The pity of war, the pity war distilled.

The Owen family at Plas Wilmot in 1895. Wilfred is sitting on his mother's knee.

Young Wilfred dressed up in a soldier suit made by his mother.

Now he is dead, bayoneted recently in battle by Owen himself. He was a German, but he is not angry or bitter. In death he forgives his former enemy and seeks reconciliation:

> I am the enemy you killed, my friend.
> I knew you in this dark: for so you frowned
> Yesterday through me as you jabbed and killed.
> I parried; but my hands were loath and cold.
> Let us sleep now . . .

A poet's youth

Wilfred Edward Salter Owen was born on 18th March 1893 at Oswestry, Shropshire. His parents were living with his grandfather, a businessman, in a large comfortable house, Plas Wilmot.

From the first his mother, Susan, was ambitious for him, carefully preserving a lock of hair of 'Sir Wilfred Edward Salter Owen at the age of 11½ months.' His father, Tom, after a never-forgotten adventurous working visit to India, now worked in a modest position as a clerk on the Great Western Railway.

When the grandfather died in 1897, the family was shocked to find that most of his capital had been spent. Plas Wilmot was sold. Tom Owen became a stationmaster in Birkenhead, Liverpool, but the family was

forced down the social scale. Their first house was in a slum district, where their feet crunched on armies of black beetles that infested it. Susan struggled to keep up middle-class appearances. Only a few pieces of family silver remained to console her.

Though not highly educated themselves, Owen's parents reared their four children, of whom Wilfred was eldest, in a cultivated atmosphere. Tom was a fine singer and a wide reader. Susan was an accomplished painter and pianist. In boyhood, Wilfred loved music and reading. 'He was always a very thoughtful imaginative child,' wrote his mother later. 'His greatest pleasure was for me to read to him even after he could read himself.'

At a time when good schooling was expensive, his family saved enough to send Wilfred to the Birkenhead Institute in 1901. He did well, showing a gift for words, and developing many interests, including a life-long passion for botany.

Keats was the poet who most inspired Wilfred. He discovered him when he was ten years old, while on holiday with his mother at Broxton in Cheshire.

Wilfred (left) riding on the sands at Scarborough, during a family holiday.

Reading in the garden of Dunsden Vicarage.

> The weeks at Broxton, by the Hill,
> Where first I felt my boyhood fill
> With uncontainable movements; there was born
> My poethood.

His mother also passed to Wilfred her deep religious feeling. He became rather a priggish youth under this influence. Sometimes, in his teens, he converted the sitting room into 'Wilfred's Church', using homemade altar cloths, surplices and bishop's mitre, while he delivered services and quite elaborate sermons.

In 1907, his father was promoted to a better post in Shrewsbury, Shropshire. Wilfred flourished at Shrewsbury Technical School, where he read widely. In his study attic, overlooking the Shropshire hills, he wrote many poems (a sackful of them were burned, at his request, by his mother after his death).

In 1911, Wilfred bought a biography of Keats. He came to identify with and almost to worship the poet. In London he saw a Keats manuscript, and told his mother 'his writing is rather large and slopes like mine.' He also saw a piece of Keats' hair:

> It is a lock of Adonais' hair!
> I dare not look too long; nor try to tell
> What glories I see glistening, glistening there.

Sadly, the lives of the two poets, Owen and Keats, were to be equally brief.

Dunsden and France

In 1911, Wilfred sat his London University Matriculation exam. He passed but did not win the scholarship he needed. He was too poor to attend university without one. Other professions—elementary school teaching, the Civil Service or journalism—were suggested to him, but his only wish was to be a poet.

Finally he followed a friend's suggestion that he should act as assistant to a country vicar. In this way he might follow his mother's wish and enter the Church. A place was found for him at Dunsden in Oxfordshire.

Wilfred stayed a year and a half in this dismal post.

Wilfred discussing poetry with the French poet Laurent Tailhade.

The vicar was an uninspiring figure, who contributed to the poet's growing belief that divinity was 'shifting, doubt-fostering, dusty and unprofitable study.' To his mother's dismay, Wilfred began to reject religion. 'I have murdered my false creed,' he told her in a letter of 1912. 'If a true one exists, I shall find it . . . Escape from this hotbed of religion I now long for.' He was impressed, however, by his visits to the local poor, and became increasingly aware of their sufferings. He described the 'wretched hovels of this parish, the crazy, evil-smelling huts of the poor.' He expressed for the first time the compassion that was the basis of his war poetry. 'From what I hear straight from the tight-pursed lips of wolfish ploughmen in their cottages, I might say there is material ready for another revolution.'

Wilfred and a cousin, Leslie Gunston, who lived nearby in Reading, formed the regular habit of writing rival poems on the same topic. Such exercises were invaluable in the long process of developing his poetic craft. Owen's early poetry showed gleams of real promise, and the strong influence of Keats. In a poem on the remains found in the Roman city of Uriconium, near his Shropshire home, he imitated Keats' manner of describing through the senses:

> Jars, whose sheen and flawless shape
> Look fresh from potter's mould.
> Plasters with Roman finger marks impressed;
> Bracelets, that from the warm Italian arm
> Might seem to be scarce cold.

His religious doubts and worries about his future brought Wilfred to a health breakdown in February 1913. To help his recovery, a doctor suggested a stay in the South of France. To his delight, he obtained a post as an English teacher at a language school in Bordeaux, and he set off in September. Wilfred enjoyed his life in France, despite long hours for little pay, and however much he exaggerated his petty illnesses in letters home (it was his lifelong habit to appeal for his mother's sympathy in this way).

41

Outbreak of war

In June 1914, Wilfred was invited to become private tutor to a wealthy family who had a summer house in the Pyrenees. He was there when the War began in August. There was 'a great stir' in the village, he told his family. 'Women were weeping all about; work was suspended. Nearly all the men have already departed . . . I feel shamefully "out of it" here, passing my time reading the newspapers in an armchair in a shady garden.' In his youthful, carefree conceit, he felt 'that the guns will effect a little useful weeding.' His first war poem was a strange contrast to his later pieces:

> Fair days are yet left for the old
> And children's cheeks are ruddy,
> Because the good lads' limbs are cold
> And their brave cheeks are bloody.

He visited a local hospital to see the war wounded and sent a detailed, and illustrated, description home, telling his brother Harold that it was 'to educate you to the actualities of the war.'

Wilfred lingered in France, tutoring another family, until September 1915. Then, although he had decided 'the fullest life liveable was a poet's', he came home to join the Army. He had seen a poster for the romantic-sounding Artists' Rifles, which offered commissions to

'Over the top' from the Somme Battle film, 1916.
Wilfred went to the Front just after the Battle ended.

re **YOU** in this?

Stirring posters like this helped to persuade Wilfred to join the army in 1915.

'any gentleman returning home from abroad.' 'I don't want to wear khaki,' he told his mother, 'nor yet to save my honour before inquisitive grandchildren fifty years hence. But I now do most intensely want to fight.'

He enlisted in London in October. The boredom of drill in London squares was relieved by visits to the famous Poetry Bookshop, run by the poet Harold Monro. He went for further training to Hare Hall Camp, Essex, and having passed his exam in May 1916, he became a Second Lieutenant in the Manchester Regiment.

Battle Experience

On New Year's Day 1917, Wilfred was in France, lying awake 'in a windy forest in the middle of a vast, dreadful encampment', the British Base at Étaples. Although he felt a 'fine, heroic feeling', he realized later that the camp was only a 'kind of paddock where the beasts are kept a few days before the shambles.'

He went to the Front, just after the Somme Battle had ended. Posted to the Beaumont Hamel sector, scene of bitter fighting in July and November 1916, he was overwhelmed by the hideous landscape. No-Man's Land was 'pock-marked like a body of foulest disease, and its odour the breath of cancer.' It was 'like the face of the moon . . . the abode of madness.' There was 'not a sign of

The appalling devastated landscape of No-Man's Land.

This painting, 'Paths of Glory' by C. R. W. Nevinson, shows dead British soldiers caught on the barbed wire of No-Man's Land.

life on the horizon, and a thousand signs of death. Not a blade of grass, not an insect; once or twice a day the shadow of a big hawk scenting carrion.' He was depressed by the blinding of one of his sentries (his poem *The Sentry* describes this) and by the dead, unburied in the bitter weather. 'We sit with them all day, all night . . . and a week later to come back and find them still sitting there, in motionless groups, that is what saps the soldierly spirit.'

At Easter Wilfred joined the British advance on the Hindenburg Line near St. Quentin. He described the sensation of going 'over the top' in an attack: 'There was an extraordinary exultation in the act of walking slowly forward . . . I kept up a kind of chanting sing-song: keep the line straight! Not so fast on the left! . . . When I looked back and saw the ground all crawling and wormy with wounded bodies, I felt no horror at all, but only an immense exultation at having got through the barrage.' When a huge shell burst near him, he was badly shell-shocked, becoming tremulous and confused. He was sent back to England, given six months' rest and posted to Craiglockhart Hospital, Edinburgh, where Siegfried Sassoon was also a patient.

Craiglockhart and the meeting with Sassoon

Battle experiences had changed Wilfred. He now believed all violence to be wrong. He wrote to his mother: 'Passivity at any price! Suffer dishonour and disgrace; but never resort to arms. Be bullied, be outraged, be killed; but do not kill.' His meeting with Siegfried Sassoon was to be a turning point in his life. Siegfried gave him the encouragement and some of the method he needed to express his new ideas in verse.

Wilfred had admired Sassoon's *The Old Huntsman*. In mid-August, he timidly knocked at his fellow patient's door, intending to ask Siegfried to sign some copies of his book. Sassoon later recalled his first glimpse of Owen: 'Short, dark-haired and shyly hesitant', he spoke with a slight stammer, in a 'rather velvety voice.' Sassoon also looked through Owen's verses, finding nothing remarkable at first, and advising him 'to sweat your guts out writing poetry.'

Wilfred set to work. He tried to use Sassoon's satirical style, but soon evolved his own methods. The manuscript of *Anthem for Doomed Youth* shows many corrections by Sassoon—he substituted 'doomed' for 'dead' in the title, for example. But it was nevertheless a revelation to Sassoon, who began to see that Owen was a much greater poet than he had previously realized. *Dulce et Decorum est* was another poem of immense power. Both Sassoon and Owen hated Jessie Pope, a writer of popular jingles for *The Daily Mail*:

> Who's for the game, the biggest that's played,
> The red crashing game of a fight?
> Who'll grip and tackle the job unafraid?
> And who thinks he'd rather sit tight?

Owen's poem 'Dulce et Decorum est' describes the effects on men of poison gas, used on the Western Front.

45

Detail from John Sargent's painting 'Gassed—scene at a dressing station . . .' Owen's poem 'The Sentry' describes the horror of the blinding of a soldier.

Opposite *Wilfred with the son of friends, photographed while on leave from the Front.*

She is 'my friend' to whom the poem is addressed. Owen answers the old Latin proverb, 'Dulce et decorum est pro patria mori' (it is sweet and fitting to die for your country) which was much quoted in the Great War, by detailing the death of a soldier at the Front, who chokes in poison gas. Owen uses ugly words and images to impress the reader with the facts of modern warfare, and to deny that there is glory in fighting. Sentimentalists would not continue giving out the old lies,

> If in some smothering dreams you too could pace
> Behind the wagon that we flung him in,
> And watch the white eyes writhing in his face . . .
> If you could hear, at every jolt, the blood
> Come gargling from the froth-corrupted lungs . . .

A year of great poetry

Wilfred left Craiglockhart in October 1917, transformed in health and prospects. 'You have fixed me,' he told Sassoon. 'I spun round you a satellite for a month, but I shall swing out soon, a dark star.'

Posted for home service, first to Scarborough, and later to Ripon, where he rented a small cottage, Owen embarked on his great elegies—*Strange Meeting, The Send-Off, Futility, Exposure, Insensibility, Miners*—in a creative period that can only be compared with the 'wonderful year' of his beloved Keats. Some of the verse bore the marks of other men's influences. But in *Futility* he found his own voice, experimenting boldly with half-rhyme, a sort of echo effect. When a soldier is shot beside him in the trench, the poet broods on the uselessness of life that can be so easily and quickly destroyed. Why did life on earth evolve at all, if it is so fragile?

> Are limbs, so dear achieved, are sides,
> Full-nerved, still warm,—too hard to stir?
> Was it for this the clay grew tall?
> —O, what made fatuous sunbeams toil
> To break earth's sleep at all?

In London, thanks to Sassoon, Wilfred met many literary men, among them the soldier poet, Osbert Sitwell, who later remembered 'the message of his eyes—deep in colour and dark in their meaning—a love of life and a poet's enjoyment of air and light.' Owen saw his first poems published (in *The Nation*) and was encouraged to plan a book. 'I am started,' he told his mother. 'The tugs have left me; I feel the great swelling of the open sea taking my galleon.'

Return to France

Owen had been depressed by the German March offensive of 1918: 'They are dying again at Beaumont Hamel, which already in 1916 was cobbled with skulls.' Hearing of Sassoon's return to the Line, he decided to go back himself. He now wanted to speak for the sufferings of the troops. His poem, *The Calls*, ends:

'Cemetary at Étaples' by John Lavery.

For leaning out last midnight on my sill
I heard the sighs of men, that have no skill
To speak of their distress, no, nor the will!
A voice I know. And this time I must go.

He crossed to France in September. The Germans were now retreating after their breakthrough. Before going to the Front, Wilfred sent Sassoon his last complete poem, the beautiful *Spring Offensive*.

In fierce fighting near St. Quentin, Wilfred Owen proved his courage, winning the Military Cross for 'conspicuous gallantry.' Although he told his mother 'My nerves are in perfect order', he wrote to Sassoon: 'My senses are charred. I shall feel again as soon as I dare but now I must not. I don't take the cigarette out of my mouth when I write "Deceased" over their letters.'

At the end of October, Wilfred wrote his final letter home, delighting in his comrades. Despite the 'ghastly glimmering of the guns outside', he told his family: 'Of this I am certain—you could not be visited by a band of friends half so fine as surround me here.'

On 4th November, near dawn, the Manchesters tried to cross the Sambre Canal near Ors. Under ferocious fire, Wilfred was seen walking among his men, encouraging them. As he helped with some duck-boards at the water's edge, he was shot and killed. There was a tragic fitness in his burial among the men whose poetic spokesman he had been.

Seven days later, on 11th November, the War ended and the guns fell silent. His parents received the dreaded telegram announcing his death as the victory bells were ringing in Shrewsbury. Because of the hysteria of the Armistice, his friends did not hear of his death for some weeks. Osbert Sitwell could only regret the waste: Owen had 'disappeared into the grey mists of those autumnal regions which had swallowed so many young lives.'

Dates and events

1893 Born in Plas Wilmot, Oswestry, Shropshire, England (18th March).

1897 Sale of Plas Wilmot. The Owens move to Birkenhead, near Liverpool.

1901 Owen goes to Birkenhead Institute.

1907 Family move to Shrewsbury, Shropshire. Owen attends Shrewsbury Technical School.

1911 Matriculates at London University. He cannot afford to attend university and becomes lay assistant to Vicar at Dunsden, Oxfordshire.

1913 After illness, goes to teach at Berlitz School, Bordeaux, France.

1914 July: becomes private tutor to French family, staying with them in the Pyrenees. August: outbreak of war.

1915 September: returns to England. October: enlists in Artists' Rifles. Training in Essex.

1916 June: commissioned in Manchester Regiment. December: moves to France.

1917 Service on Somme near Beaumont Hamel. April: shell-shocked during British Offensive near St. Quentin. July: evacuated to England. Sent to Craiglockhart Hospital, Edinburgh. August: meets Siegfried Sassoon. Begins great sequence of war poems. October: discharged from hospital. Goes to Scarborough, Yorkshire for home service.

1918 January: *Miners* published in *The Nation*. March: continued home service in Ripon, Yorkshire. Several of his best war poems written here. June: graded fit for service. *Futility* published in *The Nation*. July: Sassoon wounded. Owen decides to return to France. September: rejoins Manchesters in the Line. October: awarded Military Cross. Killed November 4th during assault on Sambre Canal, Ors, France. November 11th: end of Great War. Parents hear of death.

1920 First collection of Owen's poems published, edited by Siegfried Sassoon.

Isaac Rosenberg

Poet and painter against all odds

They left this dead with the older dead,
Stretched at the crossroads.
Burnt black by strange decay,
Their sinister faces lie
The lid over each eye,
The grass and coloured clay
More motion have than they,
Joined to the great sunk silences.

from *Dead Man's Dump* (1917)

Isaac Rosenberg disappeared on 1st April 1918, during the chaos of the mighty German offensive that began on the Western Front in late March. Not until 1926 could the authorities tell his family that his body had been found, and even now it is possible that the remains buried beneath his headstone, marked with the Jewish star and inscription 'Artist and poet', are not actually Rosenberg's.

This wretched end seemed a fitting climax to what was, on the surface, a dismal, restricted life. Unlike his fellow war poets, Rosenberg was unprepossessing: small, ugly, mumbling in his speech. Having escaped briefly from the poverty of his London East End boyhood, he was trapped again in his long war service as a private in France. He had none of the benefits of the officer's life. He wrote his poems in or near the Front Line, in conditions so grim that he complained in his last months that 'I seem even to forget words.'

Yet two qualities shine from Rosenberg's life story. The first is a determination never to give in to difficulties. In 1911, he wrote to a friend 'However hard one's lot is, one ought to try and accommodate oneself to the conditions . . . Why not make the very utmost of our lives?' The second is his devotion to his twin arts, painting and writing. His poetry at least he never gave up, even in the misery of the trenches. 'I am determined,' he wrote in 1916, 'that this war, with all its powers for devastation, shall not master my poeting.'

Victorian Bristol, where the Rosenbergs settled after leaving Russia, and where Isaac was born and spent his early years.

The Rosenbergs' shop in St George's Street, in the East End of London.

Growing up in the East End

Rosenberg's father, Dovber (or Barnett, as he called himself in England) was a Lithuanian Jew, who had fled to England in 1885, to escape military service in the Russian Army. He eventually settled in Bristol, making a poor living as a peddler. His wife Hacha joined him in 1888.

Isaac was born in Bristol on 25th November 1890, his male twin dying at birth. In 1897, with five children to provide for, the Rosenbergs moved to London, hoping to find a better life. The squalor of the Jewish Quarter in the East End was a great shock to them. Cable Street, where they lived, near the Docks, was particularly bad, with drunken sailors, beggars, and terrifying rats from the Thames warehouses. They lived in a single room between a rag and bone shop and a railway. The family only survived with the help of Jewish charities, set up to help poor immigrants.

Isaac was educated at local state-run Elementary Board Schools. Special lessons in Hebrew and Jewish worship were provided for the large number of Jewish children. Isaac hated these, although he always loved the legends of the Old Testament. At home, from an early age, he drew on scraps of paper, or with chalk on pavements, where passers-by were surprised to see their likenesses quickly sketched. His understanding head-

Isaac as a young boy.

master noticed his artistic gifts and allowed him to leave class to sit in his study, drawing and writing as he chose. A fellow pupil remembered seeing Isaac standing at the study window, gazing absorbed at a painting he had just finished. Later he attended art evening classes in Stepney.

In 1900, the Rosenbergs moved to more spacious rooms in Jubilee Street. Isaac's parents did not get on well: Hacha, who struggled to support the family by sewing, washing and fine embroidery, despised Barnett, who was lazy. Their disunity probably accounted for Isaac's gloominess as a boy.

Education at evening class

When he was fourteen, in 1905, Isaac left school to be apprenticed to a Fleet Street engraver. He never liked his work, as it gave him little time for his own art. After some years of it, he wrote to a friend: 'It is horrible to think that all these hours, when my days are full of vigour and my hands and soul craving for self-expression, I am bound, chained to this fiendish mangling-machine . . . and the days go by.'

Mile End Road, in London's East End. Isaac and other East End Jewish boys used to walk here in the evenings, discussing literature and painting.

Edward Marsh, patron of poets and painters, published a collection of Georgian poetry in 1911. He encouraged Isaac with his painting and poetry.

The work did, however, give him a small income. He enrolled for evening painting classes at Birkbeck College. He worked at his pictures in every spare moment. He also bought cheap books at Farringdon Street Market. In this way he discovered Keats, Byron and Shelley, though he identified himself with a particular hero, the struggling, poverty-stricken London poet, Francis Thompson.

Evening walks in the streets were the only entertainment for East End Jewish boys. On such walks, in 1911, Isaac made friends with other poor, clever young men like himself. One, Joseph Leftwich, kept a diary. He recorded that once at a street corner, 'Rosenberg pulls a bundle of odd scraps of paper out of his pocket and reads us poems under a lamp-post. The fellow really writes good poetry.' His writing was a contrast with his mumbling speech. 'I find it difficult to make myself intelligible at times . . . I think I leave the impression of being a rambling idiot,' Isaac said of himself. It was at this time, too, that he met Sonia Cohen, an attractive orphan girl, whom he was to paint and to whom he poured out (with little success) his most powerful love poems.

A stroke of luck

When he finished his apprenticeship in March 1911, Isaac, confident in his artistic powers, decided to be an artist rather than an engraver. To his close friend and adviser, a teacher called Winifred Seaton, he wrote: 'Congratulate me! I've cleared out of the shop . . . I'm free—free to do anything.'

Then he was lucky. One day, as he sat in the National Gallery, copying a picture in the hope of impressing the Jewish Educational Society, a wealthy Jewish lady, Lily Joseph, noticed and befriended him. In July he was amazed to hear that she and a Mrs Cohen were prepared to pay his fees at the Slade School of Art in London.

The art student

The Slade, with its superb staff of outstanding artists, was, said Isaac, 'The finest school for drawing in England.' At that time the students were full of the new painting ideas they had seen at the Post-Impressionist Exhibition of 1910. At that exhibition English audiences first saw Cezanne, Van Gogh, Gauguin and Matisse. There were brilliant Slade students too: Paul Nash, Stanley Spencer, William Roberts, C. R. W. Nevinson—who all later became well-known war artists—and two 'Whitechapel Boys' from Rosenberg's own Jewish background, Mark Gertler and David Bomberg. Isaac, less interested in experimental painting than in making a living from his art, was a quiet student among many flamboyant personalities. 'I do nothing but draw—draw—' he told Miss Seaton.

Despite his efforts, Isaac had little success as a painter. His picture *Joy* won a prize certificate in a Slade competition. He had a few paintings exhibited in South Kensington and Whitechapel. And, after a meeting arranged by his friend Gertler, he did sell a charming work, *Sacred Love,* to Edward Marsh, who thereafter became a friend and patron.

Isaac (far left) with fellow Slade art students

55

Rosenberg was a talented artist. This painting of a friend, Sonia Rodker, hangs in a London gallery.

Opposite *Ambulances collecting the wounded from Charing Cross Station: detail from the painting by J. Hodgson Lobley.*

When he left the Slade in March 1914, Isaac was already thought of by his friends more as a poet than as a painter. Two years before, he had published at his own expense a pamphlet of poems, *Night and Day*. He sent it to a well-known poet, Laurence Binyon, for comment. Binyon recorded his impressions of his subsequent meeting with Rosenberg who was 'small in stature, dark, bright-eyed, thoroughly Jewish in type . . . Possessed of vivid enthusiasms, he was shy in speech . . . There was an odd charm in his manner, which came from his earnest transparent sincerity.' Binyon found his poems unusual and 'at times there gushed forth a pure song which haunted the memory.'

Rosenberg's poetry changed under the influence of the poet-painter William Blake, whose works he saw at a 1913 exhibition, and he began writing his first mature verse.

Journey to South Africa

Isaac's health declined during his time at Art School. Partly for this reason and also to escape the pain of his unrequited love for Sonia Cohen, he decided to go to South Africa. His sister Minnie had settled in Cape Town after her recent marriage. He planned to teach or work on a farm, while he developed his painting and his poetry. Edward Marsh helped with the fare, and Isaac arrived in Cape Town in June 1914. 'The place is gorgeous,' he wrote home, relishing the hot climate, and what to him was the astonishing respect he was given as an artist. He soon found a number of painting commissions in Cape Town. After hearing the news of the Declaration of War he wrote to Edward Marsh in August 1914: 'I despise and hate war.' He seemed far away from the conflict and detached from it. Yet, in a powerful poem, *On Receiving News of the War,* he sensed how everyone's life would be changed by it:

> . . . Some spirit old
> Hath turned with malign kiss
> Our lives to mould . . .

Enlistment

Reluctantly, Isaac came back to England in February 1915. He was again uncertain about his future, unable to support himself or find work. Guilty at having to live off his family, the Army, with its guaranteed shilling a day, tempted him. He told the American poet, Ezra Pound: 'There is certainly a strong temptation to join when you are making no money.' Finally, leaving home without telling his family, Rosenberg enlisted in the Army in late October 1915.

Too short to enter a regular regiment, Isaac joined the strange Bantam Battalion, formed specially for undersized men. He was posted at once to Bury St. Edmunds, Suffolk. The Battalion seemed 'the most rascally affair in the world', full of recruits like 'Falstaff's scarecrows.' Isaac found himself eating from a basin 'with some horribly smelling scavenger who spits and sneezes into it.' Typically, he had absent-mindedly joined up with no belongings, and had to train in his one suit, and dry himself on a pocket handkerchief. When he told his parents about enlisting, they were deeply shocked.

Training was misery. Stiff boots hurt his feet, causing him 'horrible pain.' He was bullied by 'a little impudent school pup for an officer.' And he was subjected to anti-Jewish prejudice. His absent-mindedness—he was planning poems in his head—brought him heavy punishments. Isaac soon began to feel that 'nobody but a private in the Army knows what it is to be a slave.'

Near the Front Line: 'A working party watching artillery fire' by A. Hill.

Transferred in March 1916, to a better regiment, the King's Own Royal Lancasters, he was soon ready for France. During his last leave Isaac arranged for a private printing of his verse play, *Moses.* Then, not daring to tell his parents, he said goodbye to his sister Annie through the wire fence of Aldershot Camp, and left for the Front.

Last months in France

Except for ten days leave in 1917, Isaac Rosenberg spent the remainder of his life in France. His short letters do not try to describe his war experiences. He only gives hints: there are 'the huge and terrible sensations of sinking in the mud.' He sees 'horrible things' like 'dead buried men blown out of their graves.' Trench fatigues are 'dull, stupefying labour' and winter 'is not least of the horrors of war.' Thanks to Marsh's

Isaac and his brother on leave in 1917.

Isaac described the nightmare of sinking in Flanders mud at the Front.

intervention he spent some months as a clerk in safe areas, but he was very often in or near the trench lines.

Rosenberg continued to think mostly about his poetry, even in this war world where 'death seems to underlie even our underthoughts.' Although Marsh was baffled by the difficulty of his poems, another poet, Gordon Bottomley, who later became his first editor, praised his work warmly in a letter. The poet soon determined to write about the War: 'I will saturate myself with the strange and extraordinary new conditions of this life, and it will refine itself into poetry later.'

He sent poems home to his various patrons, despite an order not to 'as the censor can't be bothered with going through such rubbish.' *Break of Day in the Trenches* was one of these. It is about the fragility of men in the front line. They are slaves or 'bonds to the whims of murder' and are 'sprawled in the bowels of the earth.' They are short-lived, like the poppies that bloom on the trench parapets. The rat that crosses No-Man's Land has more freedom and dignity than the soldiers.

Dead Man's Dump was written while Isaac was working on the supply carts taking stores to the

Exhausted British soldiers in the trenches: Rosenberg wrote some of his finest poetry in these terrible conditions.

Manuscript of 'Break of Day in the Trenches'.

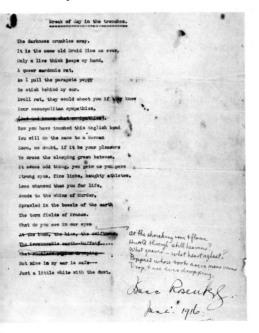

trenches. Sometimes they ran over dead bodies, heaped for burial at the roadside:

> The wheels lurched over sprawled dead
> But pained them not, though their bones crunched.
> Their shut mouths made no moan,
> They lie there huddled, friend and foeman
> Man born of man, and born of woman,
> And shells go crying over them
> From night till night and now.

This horrific experience makes the poet reflect on the mystery of death. Where has life gone from the bodies?

> None saw their spirit's shadow shake the grass,
> Or stood aside for the half-used life to pass
> Out of those doomed nostrils and the doomed mouth.

He watches as a man recently dead is thrown onto the pile of corpses. Like them, this man is now joined to the 'great sunk silences' of death.

During his last months, Isaac made repeated requests to join the Jewish Battalion, which was formed from Jewish emigrants from Russia. In 1918, the Battalion was fighting in Egypt and Palestine. His requests were not accepted and, disappointed, he wrote his poem, *Through these pale cold days*, in which the idea of Jews in exile from Palestine is related to any soldier's hopeless longing to return home:

> They leave these blond still days
> In dust behind their tread.
> They see with living eyes
> How long they have been dead.

Having 'bagged an inch of candle' in the trenches to write it by, he sent it home to Marsh. It was his last poem —he was dead before the letter crossed the Channel.

On the evening of 31st March 1918, Rosenberg's unit was in the Front Line, at Fampoux, near Arras, facing the overwhelming German offensive that had begun ten days before. Early on 1st April, the survivors were sent back behind the lines to rest. On their way back, volunteers were called for to resist a renewed German attack. Isaac returned to the battle, and was killed in the fighting, no one quite knows how. After some days, he was buried in a mass grave.

A dead soldier: 'Gassed' by G. Rogers.

Dates and events

1890 Born in Bristol, son of Jewish emigrants from Russia.

1897 Family moves to Cable Street in the East End of London. Isaac enters the local Elementary Board School.

1902 Given special art and writing classes at his school.

1904 Leaves school: apprenticed to firm of engravers.

1907 Attends art evening class at Birkbeck College.

1911 Finishes apprenticeship and decides to live as an artist. Meets Lily Joseph. She and Mrs Cohen pay his fees at the Slade School of Art, London.

1911 October: joins the Slade.

1912 *Night and Day* poetry booklet published privately.

1913 November: meets Edward Marsh, one of several patrons who helped him.

1914 March: leaves Slade. June: sails to Cape Town, to stay with sister. Aug: Britain declares war on Germany.

1915 February: returns to England. April: privately publishes *Youth*, a poetry booklet . October: enlists as private in Bantam Battalion. Trains at Bury St. Edmunds, Suffolk.

1916 March: transfers to King's Own Royal Lancasters Regiment. May: *Moses* privately published. June: arrives in France. August: goes into Trenches on the Somme. December: *Break of Day in the Trenches* published in American Magazine *Poetry*.

1917 Service in France. Fragment from *Moses* published in Marsh's *Georgian Poetry 1916-17*.

1918 April: Rosenberg is killed during German offensive near Arras. Buried at Fampoux.

1922 *Poems by Isaac Rosenberg* published.

1937 *Collected Works* published (edited by G. Bottomley and D. Harding). Foreward by Siegfried Sassoon.

1979 *Collected Works* published.

Glossary

Armistice A suspension of fighting in a war.

Battalion A unit of an army (about 800 men in British Army battalion of Great War).

Commission The rank of an officer in the Army.

Conscientious objector Someone who objects to army service on the grounds of conscience.

Court martial A military court that tries offences against army law.

Draft Soldiers being transported to war front or conscripted for military service.

Elegy A poem of sorrow or mourning.

Half rhyme Rhymes that are not exact but which give an echo: for instance, tall/toil, star/stir, now/ know.

Jingle A catchy rhyme or verse.

Manuscript The hand-written version of a poem or book.

No-Man's Land The area between the trench lines of opposing sides in the Great War.

Pacifist Someone who is totally against war and violence.

Patron Someone who gives money, opportunity or encouragement to a writer or artist.

Satire Writing which mocks wicked or foolish qualities of society, making them appear ridiculous.

Shell-shock Nervous exhaustion brought about by bombardment in the trenches.

Sonnet Fourteen-line poem of a particular rhyme and rhythm scheme.

Volunteer Someone who offers to serve without being asked to do so.

Further reading

If you would like to find out more about the First World War and about these four poets, you may like to read the following books:

On the War:

All Quiet on the Western Front by Erich Maria Remarque (Heinemann/New Windmill)

Battle of the Somme by Christopher Martin (Wayland 1973)

First World War Atlas by Michael Gilbert (Weidenfeld and Nicolson 1970)

Goodbye to All That by Robert Graves (Penguin 1960)

Testament of Youth by Vera Brittain (Virago 1978)

On Rupert Brooke:

Poetical Works edited by Geoffrey Keynes (Faber and Faber 1974)

Rupert Brooke: A Biography by Christopher Hassall (Faber and Faber 1964)

On Wilfred Owen:

War Poems and Others edited by W. Hibberd (Chatto and Windus 1973)

Wilfred Owen: A Biography by Jon Stallworthy (Oxford University Press 1974)

On Siegfried Sassoon:

Collected Poems (Faber and Faber 1961)

The Complete Memoirs of George Sherston by Siegfried Sassoon (Faber and Faber 1937)

On Isaac Rosenberg:

The Collected Works of Isaac Rosenberg edited by I. Parsons (Chatto and Windus 1979)

Journey to the Trenches: The Life of Isaac Rosenberg by J. Cohen (Robson Books 1975)

On war poetry:

First World War Poetry edited by Jon Silkin (Penguin 1979)

Poets of the First World War by Jon Stallworthy (Oxford University Press 1974)

The English Poets of the First World War by John Lehmann (Thames and Hudson 1981)

Up the Line to Death edited by Bryan Gardner (Methuen 1964)

Index

Antwerp landing 14
Armistice, the 34, 49
Asquith, Violet 16

Battles of:
Passchendaele 22
The Somme 21, 26-7, 42, 43
Binyon, Lawrence 56

Brooke, Rupert 7-19
birth and childhood 9
at Rugby School 9
appearance 9, 10, 14
at Kings College, Cambridge
9, 10, 11
interest in drama 9
interest in Fabianism 9
influence of John Donne 10
moves to Grantchester 11
first collection of poems
published 11
love affair with 'Ka' Cox 12
wins Fellowship at Kings 12
visits America and the South
Seas 13
stays in Tahiti 13
meets Sassoon 14
joins Royal Naval Division 14
battle experience 14
writes war sonnets 15
sails for Gallipoli 15-16
becomes ill 17
death 17
buried on Skyros 16, 17
poems:
A Channel Passage 11
Peace 7, 15
*The Old Vicarage,
Grantchester* 11
The Soldier 7, 15
Tiare Tahiti 13
Churchill, Winston 7, 14, 21
Cohen, Sonia 54, 56
Cornford, Frances 15

Cox, Katherine 12

Davies, W.H. 25
Dean Inge 7,8

Gallipoli 8, 17, 18
Garsington Manor 30, 34
Georgian Poetry 26, 31
Graves, Robert 26, 31

Hardy, Thomas 5, 22

Marsh, Edward 11, 12, 25, 54,
55, 56, 59
Masefield, John 25
Morrell, Lady Ottoline 30

Nash, Paul 22, 55
Nesbitt, Cathleen 12, 14
Nicholls, Robert 33
No-Man's Land 21, 33, 43, 44

Owen, Wilfred 37-49
birth and childhood 38
poverty 38-9
education 39, 40
inspired by John Keats 39, 40,
41, 47
religious feelings 40
assists Vicar of Dunsden
40-41
rejects religion 41
suffers health breakdown 41
becomes teacher in France
41-2
enlists in the Army 42-3
sent to the Front 43
sent home shell-shocked 44-5
goes to Craiglockhart
Hospital 45-6
meets Sassoon 45-6
appearance 45
writes elegies 47

courage in action 48
wins Military Cross 48
death 49
poems:
Anthem for Doomed Youth 45
Dulce et Decorum est 45
Exposure 47
Futility 47
Insensibility 47
Miners 47
Spring Offensive 48
Strange Meeting 37, 47
The Calls 47
The Send-Off 47
The Sentry 44, 46
The Soldier 7, 18

Poison gas 28, 45, 46, 61
Pope, Jessie 45

Rosenberg, Isaac 51-60
appearance 5, 56
birth and childhood 52, 53
life in London's East End 52
education 52, 53
love of Old Testament 52
artistic gifts noticed 53
attends art classes 53
works as engraver 53
draws and paints 54, 55
love for Sonia Cohen 54
befriended by Lily Joseph 54
attends Slade School 55
influence of William Blake 56
visits South Africa 56
joins Bantam Battalion 57
transfers to Kings Own Royal
Lancasters 58
goes to the Front 58
death 60
poems:
Break of Day in the Trenches
59, 60

Rosenberg, Isaac *(continued)*
  Dead Man's Dump 46, 51
  Moses 58
  Night and Day 56
  On Receiving News of the War
    56
  Through these pale cold days
    60

Rugby School 9, 18
Russell, Bertrand 30

Sassoon, Siegfried 31-35
  birth and childhood 23
  at Marlborough College 24
  studies at Clare College,
    Cambridge 25
  enjoys fox-hunting 23, 24
  writes poetry as a hobby 24
  meets Brooke 25

enlists in Yeomanry 26
obtains commission in Royal
  Welch Fusiliers 26
goes to the Front 26
courage in action 26
wins Military Cross 27
starts writing angry war
  poems 29
wounded and shell-shocked
  29
makes statement of protest
  against the War 30, 31
sent to Craiglockhart Hospital
  31-2
meets Owen 32
publishes *Counter Attack* 32
poems:
  Died of Wounds 28
  Everyone Sang 34

Memoirs of an Infantry Officer
  28, 29
The Daffodil Murderer 25
The General 30
The Hero 29
The Old Century 23
The Old Huntsman 29, 45

Seaton, Winifred 54, 55
Sitwell, Osbert 47
Skyros 17, 18

Trenches 5, 21, 27, 32, 52, 58-9,
  60

War Requiem 37
Webb, Beatrice and Sidney 9
Wells, H. G. 9, 30, 35
Western Front 2, 21, 45, 51
Woolf, Virginia 10

Picture acknowledgements

The publishers would like to thank all those who provided illustrations on the following pages: BBC Hulton Picture Library 8 (lower), 26, 31 (lower), 52 (top), 53 (lower), 54; Fitzwilliam Museum 20, 30 (top); Imperial War Museum *front cover*, 4, 16 (top), 22, 27, 28, 31 (top), 32 (top and lower), 33, 38 (top and lower) 39, 40, 41, 42, 43 (top and lower), 44, 46, 47, 48, 50 (lower), 53 (top), 55, 56, 57, 58, 59 (top and lower), 60 (top and lower), 61; Keystone Press Agency 23; Kings College, Cambridge 6, 8 (top), 9, 10 (lower), 11 (upper and lower), 12 (lower), 15, 16 (lower), 17, 18 (top and lower); Mansell Collection 45; Mary Evans Picture Library 25, 34; National Portrait Gallery 36; John Topham Picture Library 13 (top), 19, 24.